I0605893

Praise

"Conor Mc Donnell's *What We Know So Far Is ...* is a brilliant tangle of lyrics and logos, a wild simulacrum of the poet's thoughts about a 'haptic universe' – one we can perceive through the body, one that we can feel. This long poem is equally concerned with thought and feeling, with biology and memes, with the murmuration of birds and the susurration of words we whisper silently to ourselves but that we wish for others to hear. In the hunt for things unseen, and in the placing of lines on paper, sometimes beautiful, sometimes fantastical, sometimes contradictory, Mc Donnell's epic looks beyond the wasteland of human existence and recalibrates not just our relationship to language, but also to nature, and to ourselves."

– Chris Banks, author of ***Alternator*** and ***Deepfake Serenade***

"Blending references to medicine and zombie movies, to *Donnie Darko* and anatomy, to internet meme culture and the musicality of Radiohead, Joy Division and the Pixies, *What We Know So Far Is ...* asks us to consider both the power and futility of words in connecting us – to our past and future selves, to each other, and to the earth."

– Paola Ferrante, author of ***Her Body Among Animals***

"An electric current runs through this poem and part of the speaker's challenge is to 'isolate silence first.' Edgy and vast, grounded in body, in biology, in physics, this poem stretches the dimensions of life and death confronting the line between. *What We Know So Far Is ...* a visionary, kaleidoscopic cry."

– Catherine Graham, author of ***Put Flowers Around Us and Pretend We're Dead***

"McDonnell mines late-modernism to give us this stream-of-consciousness epic, in the tradition of TS Eliot and JH Prynne, that is at once lyrical and abstract, formal yet playful."

– James Lindsay, author of ***Only Insistence*** and ***Double Self-Portrait***

"*What We Know So Far Is ...* a book of vocal assemblings and disassemblings. Equipped with a brilliantly expansive set of cultural allusions, Mc Donnell gets his hands deep beneath the superficiality of language, and then he just starts twisting. The result is a challenging book, eager to press and interrogate. But it's also an improbably joyful one as the poet uncovers new ideas in the folding and unfolding words as he quests for their sharper historical cores. This is a book that poses ample questions, and while the answers are elusive, it is positively giddy about the chase."

– Jacob McArthur Mooney, author of ***Frank's Wing*** and ***The Northern***

what we know so far is ...

Also by Conor Mc Donnell

Poetry
Recovery Community
This Insistent List

Chapbooks
The Book of Retaliations
In the Museum
Safe Spaces

what we know so far is ...

Conor Mc Donnell

Published by Buckrider Books
an imprint of Wolsak and Wynn Publishers
280 James Street North
Hamilton, ON L8R2L3
www.wolsakandwynn.ca

Editor: Paul Vermeersch | Copy editor: Ashley Hisson
Cover and Interior design: Kilby Smith-McGregor
Author photograph: Omii Thompson
Typeset in Minion Pro and Real Head Pro
Printed by Coach House Printing Company, Toronto, Canada

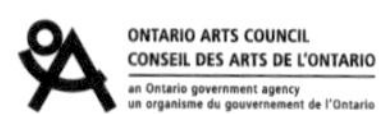

Canada

The publisher gratefully acknowledges the support of the Canada Council for the Arts and the Ontario Arts Council. We also acknowledge the financial support of the Government of Canada through the Canada Book Fund and the Government of Ontario through the Ontario Book Publishing Tax Credit and Ontario Creates.

Library and Archives Canada Cataloguing in Publication

Title: What we know so far is... / Conor Mc Donnell.
Names: Mc Donnell, Conor, 1970- author.
Identifiers: Canadiana 20250274957 | ISBN 9781998408269 (softcover)
Subjects: LCGFT: Poetry.
Classification: LCC PS8625.A2315 W43 2025 | DDC C811/.6—dc23

This book is for Audrey Jeudy, Patrice Mc Donnell, Imelda Gallagher & Fiona O'Donnell,

proof (if you really need it) that Valkyries walk among us

Prologue

Nulla

"Can't you tell by my accent? I'm speaking your language, man! But you can't speak my language, because I was in the hole before you. But you'll speak the language of the next person who falls in."

– Hassan Blasim, "The Hole"

The dimension of an object is defined as the minimum number of coordinates needed to specify any one point within it. A line has a dimension of one [1D], a surface, e.g., a square, has a dimension of two [2D] because two coordinates are needed to specify a point upon it, etc. Another way to consider dimension is as n-1. A 2D square is bounded by 1D lines, whereas a 3D cube is bounded by 2D areas, therefore a 4D object, e.g., a tesseract, the hyper surface of which is represented by eight cubical cells, is bounded by 3D volumes. In order to construct the "next" dimension up, we are restricted by the boundaries of the "current"

A communicant viral biome pervades and inhabits everything. As viruses surround us, live on us, inside us, in our air, on our pets' breath, in the lining of our blood vessels, some will extend toward communication and in order to do so such viruses will use animals and species as hosts. They enter the host to subtly alter it in order to foster trans-species communication. In some circumstances the host cannot support the geometry of altered language, nor can it tolerate the dissonance foist upon its internal inaudible hum: such is one way toward inevitable "madness," intolerance manifest through the host's inability to communicate effectively with "their own kind" now they straddle the syntax of more than one species. Vocabulary remains mostly recognizable, but the use to which it is put cannot be understood by those who exist beyond its boundaries, nor can we calibrate current audiology to decipher what is otherwise perceived as ramblings, flights of fancy, pressure of ideas and supposed elusions. We cannot calibrate so instead we medicate. We drown the noise around the signal but fail to perceive that which we can't measure and frame because of an inability to contain the accepted definition of a dimension, in this case the viral dimension – pioneers of which are influencers, algorithmic investors, ill-fated savants and those silent auto-immunocompromiseds

What We Know So Far Is …

I

cars crash. Omagh. Wrists are slapped. Omaha.
Nothing happens not willed in a haptic universe.

Were you to decode our red-herring DNA – escape
accumulated rubbish of omnibus *Sandman*,
Gandalf & Saruman,
Verses by Salman,
Siamese Dream on vinyl,
cassette & double CD, the
animal pets, our unarticulated selves
(the *Innominatum Os* of us) –

such loss would leave me light-headed yet,
clothed in rubble to ground me:
rough judgment pressing on raw nerve until
it's like listening to a fucking headache.

Could such stasis be wished for, lifeless words writ
onto plasmic existence? If so, silence this lisp of spirit,

steady this teleological stutter for,
sometimes I misread words …

II

Their children are grown does not scan as *their kids are now adults* to me.

My first thought: How are they razed?
Are they handpicked at birth or
pared by secateurs instead?

What We Know So Far Is …

III

The Irish for *harvest* is *Fómhar* (it also means *autumn*).
I say, Autumn,
you think, Fall,
as in: *We harvest what autumns from the trees.*

Either way, less bloodshed come time to reap:
meme protects the disease.

Let me store Fómhar in my cheeks till Spring:
this thing I've taken to building is all beauty
no bone, no anatomy,
soft-launch simulacrum of suspect mind –
Elvi and slivers of truth lit up from within
by amnesia struck on the flint of repetitive punishments.

You might liken it to bruise but
peruse the back of older pages
rough to the touch like indents
                                        pockmarked revisionist lumps
cratering inner surface of skulls where
                                            edit and idea land
and bubble up – homesick, empty and drunk –
like reverse-phrenology, nephrology deniers,
shredding filters to stem this flight of ideas,
like
throbbing skulls on stilts, like
turtles twisting over limerick's worth of worms,
like snacking serpents shook loose and spread across fields;
the itches they scratch will weep and leak …
erupt if left undisturbed.

IV

Deliverance ribs the silent vibrato of angels bent backward over scarlet alarm.

Murmuration, unleashed by the throng, prays high in beams above:
swoops & swoons over sacristy, lording over the gathered beneath,
deftly sculpting angle of descent
                         anger of dissent
                         angst of decency
                         angelic deception on auto-repent.

V

How to make absolute sense of the utterly::maybe try naming by anagram

::: *Eden* to *Need* = *Name* to *Amen* :::

This is the me theme
(the *me* in *theme*)

Hold fast to the ankh of discipline

Turn ancient words over and over again.

VI

See family huddled at the O.R. door:
their father, an organ donor,
declared brain-dead barely two hours before.
His name neatly printed on the O.R. board
but, under the heading

Procedure to be performed

one word
Harvest

scrawled in Sharpie

VII

I believe words are thirsty predators: pack hunters:
to be seen is death to the herd,
to be heard means death-en-scene.

Words cower in the long grass of language,
slip blades of whispered-phrase before striking
when the he[a]rd (ignorant & illiterate)
is seen and grammatically gored.

VIII

Fragments project a half-mile high onto thinly sketched horizons.
Wildfires kiss dark edges of town.
Tsunamis fester a few leagues down.
Ontario burns but I live by the lakefront.

Revenant words churn malignant code

:::abstract subtract extract unfold –– abstract subtract extract behold:::

::streetlamps daydream & dap moonlit skies::

:hot seas simmer to dupe the disguise:

Lewy bodies scamper family tree

to wipe out root and sapling:

.meme protects its own disease.

IX

Memes disseminate cultural genes
[*mimime*, Greek for *imitate*]
– alarmed coalitions of pronouns & values (me my & mine) –
trigger expression of me-me genes:

audible
visual
verbal & id-ible:
every last me a building block, an unwed unfed nucleotide.

Early abstraction trips replication
lost in transcription @33-glans per footage of robe –

slip us a hem to the mountain-foot,
next bone up attaches to shin,
climb up for access & come on in,
join us at ball & socket joint
of jump-cut risk reassessments,
sentence unrepentant words
to anti-speech immunity,
welcome home communicant-biome:
Prepare a link to inhibit everything. Everywhere
all at once neo-syllables surround & pre-word us
to spin out the web of our species-wide tongue.

Some of us refuse these gifts of mutation,
blame neo-configurations on blighted code:
[there are other webs but beyond this one].

Dissonance
and intolerance
is foist on infernal hum,
struck up within our resistant vessels:
intima – lumina – media – none.

X

What We Know So Far Is the first steps to madness
– manifest as ill-communication with kin –
quickly slip into species-specific syntax:
even when vocab regains recognition the filter-ware crashes
for lack of new phrasings.

Resultant flights of fantasy
(elusions piled atop pressure of ideals)
blare failures to backup & recalibrate:
demand instead we (p)re-medicate.

Our focus shifts to refit the base signal.

Anti-rejection algorithm outfits nucleolar core;

We are in the ephemera industry now.

XI

We are the ephemera industry.
Cued exponentials tag neo-quorum-physics to re-abandoned pathologies:

machine biology,
mortality clones, creation
of Innominatum machines.

Memes encode the manifest:
we build them out before they distress.

They shred teratology of letter and word:
reverse the mould to make things broken because,

Word is predator and lazy language made to pay.

When no one questions anymore, why hunt things unseen?
Can colours be trapped within drabbest word, images seared
onto crooked beams?

Might we blast Morse of flashed colour instead,
do you think we could maybe try that next? Stop
sucking the light from everything?

Our throats are obstructed by calcule-machines,
whispered code and loose-lipped spectra explode
from bottle-green equations; the countdown dissembles

one unopposable
digit at a time
...
..
.

XII

Speak time another way

Line it up like [insert your own words here].
Would you cut your own line[s], or at least
please try? But of course, you won't, right?

When I crack a word open I drift inside its organelles,
imprint, record & splice the offal – sliced permutations
the only answer to uber-countercultural hum – whisper
to the rubble that used to be the museum. Whisper

into dying books under the bricks and retellings of gospel mysteries:
Who was the Mark and who was the john?

Body of Christ possessed.
Body of Christ passed on passed up, and yes,
passed over in thrall to his first commandment.

Such relinquent powers of liberation – free-wave new-wave
next-wave-war – red-band guerrilla-fare & underground wounds –
bindings of aspiration-burns – absence of underlying silences –

these and more besides persist as strongest signal yet:

The HIGHpothesis
:Silence ∃-> License ∃-> Listen ∃-> Silent
(Cue last Abstraction & first Mutation Leap)
∃-> Virtual ∃-> Tu-Viral ∃-> TuRival
∃-> Survival: Survival from Silence
exists:

1.

what we know so far is cars crash. Oklahoma! wrists were slapped. nothings haptic willingly in an occidental universe. the underground wounds, bindings of aspiration-burns and absence of silence persist in the underlay as strongest signals yet. they misdirect and disconnect us from what we know so far: toss us onto icefields, grind the grounds to blue dust beneath us, hollow discreetly that in-between self of re(e)merge & re-rejection

1.

XIII

A portion of our disconnect misdirects us
to what we know so far as connectin,
the largest human protein (also referred to as titin).

Connectin counters muscle-bindle overstretch
to facilitate elasticity.
                    Plasticity,
the ability to make structural rearrangements,
confers extra tolerance to mutation.

One titin isoform regulates chromosomal condensation.
Cohesion-defects and mis-segregation arise from
failures to condense; does it follow
that segregation is pro-cohesion?

XIIIb

In 1955,
they spliced *Gelasinospora* to *autosteira*.
The control plates formed perithecia & segregated asci.
For every incidental combination of white & brown,
they observed four black spores form by primary intention:
these were known as ascii.

ASCII is a character-encoded electronic communication
(American Standard Code for Information Interchange).

During interphase (where cells spend most of their life cycle),
Nuclear titin (proteinaceous Enola Gay)
is essential for chromosomal stability.

Interzones stand out as suspended states between two or more occupied zones. They endure intrepid drift of medium & mode (perspective-creep from report to record); forge order from older sports. Rendered absence of confirmation breathes new life into undisturbed rubble of big-boy tantrums and creeped-out follow-ups – all-age sunrise to sunset shows, straight-edge gang crime running interference all cherry blossom and Sturm und Drang …

XIIIc

The other cheek of the past is a lie,
heart attack rehab aftermath reaching hard for contra-womb
where Christ-ian dreams are born
where
bleeding-heart clocks sit atop listed buildings
to lean in better for empath effect over those dropped hard
onto sanctuary's doorstep by daft-punk cops
                              running faster
                              cutting deeper
                              rutting harder
                              cumming lauda.

                                                  New Virgin routes launch
without median strips so newborns can outpace their
gathering dust. Their discards yield to no signage, set
off on never-where journeys tagged to imprint-tracks
up and down the back and beyond of themselves.

Press
thumb deep to staunch the flow:
Nausicaa's only cover is blown.
Newest imprint runs in reverse
until textures flex and plunge
to divert the emergent whole ...

XIIId

what we know so far is
Titin studies are restricted by protein's leviathan size so
we break it into more manageable bites. Its chemical name
– longest word laid on English tongues – is 189,819 letters
long, and takes three hours to pronounce in full.

Lexicographers troll it as formula – pas langue – because
written rules will never supplant their founding principles
of x, y and z.

What We Know So Far Is
Interzone is safe haven within which to improvise:
This is why the first burial was the first act of love,
early words set ceremony as inchoate connection
to older ways when pupils pinned & dilated at will.

Failure today to individuate confirms desperate
transplants will never take while overlaid on a
lifetime of self-rejection. The unwritten parts

(those lines unsaid) cloud mirrors of what was
intended, yet: If we do believe our ghosts leave
footprints and words are cruel sentinels, brutal

deceptions raised to feed off simple truths like
whistling down the underdog or calling across
the icefields or walking west to Mama Christ,

then maybe discrete paths will merge:
reveal the most haunted parts of us.

2.

what we know so far is cars crash underground and wrists slap haptic in an occipital universe. the absence of aspiration burns hard wounds into silence. Seveso. bindings are final signal redirecting what we used to know: how to sluice blue-ice to disconnect from underneath. hollow haunted spectacle marks best time for an Irish to show: their Gaelic gases smother liquid states: their solids and stiffs lie bested and livid.

2.

what we know so far is …

XIV

… the Irish for *ghost*, *taibhse*, means *show*,
while *taibhseach* means *showy* or *spectacular*,
and *taibhsím* means *I appear*.

Taibhsím taibhse taibhseach,
I appear as spectacular show

but also I appear as showy ghost.

Words worm their way in . . .
We screw things up to an uneasy peace,
fill it with missed opportunities:

no copy-shroom-hearts
no time to pretend
no postcard management
no cuckoo-drinks for happy-hour friends
no happy fountain sprinkling future fields
(please, do not believe everything I feel)
no toddler-tantrum planting flag
to tag near-future adulterers.

We criss-cross misplaced realities
to timeshare borders of purgatory.

XV

For angels to fly unclipped they choose
genetics over genitals every time.
The bargain to fuck or fly swaps
angelus for Apology,
water and clay for celestial strategy.

Until we deny angel-Maker's magic
satirists will flense our futures raw
and, Hallelujah,
the blind will see the tick head dug deep,
slick and sloppy as any worm.

Philologists wage forgotten phrases
primed to rise in future states. Wagers,
antidote to weaponized meme,
combat third-planet-modesty of mice-men
and collar(e)d humanities.

Old roads bang out a beat to new adventures in pornography:
Rhythm is a dancer, tipping a privilege,
good intentions stay at home. Nudie nudie
on the wall: who is the mirrorest one of all?

Staring into reflections together you never
look the same as me: I'm pegylated at best.
My pulse is at war with my tidal breath while
suffragettes shred predators' luggage
on freelance flights to hell.

Stand to for the razor-attack:
schoolboys – ever-hot to touch – close ranks to
stab and run collectives through for the killer gone,
for silent shout, for west is Brightside of morning,
for junior-fire, for arcade boys forget old liars' lies,
forged bright and buried in cleanest whiteys.

Feral parents tiptoe to water: pretty boys the same.
Shins sink fast into mud for Jesus, Pyramid, New
Age, Radio-Wu-Tang-Play & White-stripe-wolves.

Red Rover, Red Rover, send pretty boy over to shine
mausoleum of body & blood on dim sum Sundays
in glorious light of family. Send pretty boy over to

Morse our hard-won misery,
take mercy & morsel recently healed
to turn their backs on charity:
reverse on into divinity.

XVI

Do those who shell the invisible catch abandon traps of creation?
Do they fashion their own articulate selves? Does gravity practise

attract & repulse, bounce forces back & forth until fulcrum-switch
flickers, until Torquemada-chimeras charge at stereoisomers spinning
chant-singing love me hate me love me, ohhhhhmmm?

At terminal velocity equipoise is (b)reached. LaGrange coordinates
hover en-niche like digital pins pecking patiently over semiotic maps.
The manufactured absence of silence numbs from theory to hypothesis.

In denunciation-days to come there may yet be a place for us but the
names we crave are problems of our own making (lazy accounting of

self-made prophecies). Joy, selfish act of resistance, re-circumscribes
to Oi, itself an act of brutishness: and yet, what we know so far is …

XVII

… fear Trumps training every time, even when drilled to flee.

All eyes on the white coat for now, none on the chaos beneath.
Physician, heal thyself or else, Physician, simply heel instead,

to thine own sell be true.

I think a terrible thought for myself:
I am groomed to accept this high mark of progress;
there are other worlds but they hide out in this one.

Meme, please, greet my unease:
foundlings groomed in faded geometries
spin chambered wheels three-times widdershins on broadcast TV.
Curses! Wrong number. Or,
right number wrong word
(in another wor[l]d).

Once we were buried with offerings
like flowers pressed into secret diaries,
yet now we dissolve under concrete tongues marked
HERE LIES SO & SO: protest-poet, quisling-king.

The epic quest weighed down reverts to uninspired mythology:
the Venn of maze & labyrinth keeps disrepair & protest comfy.

The maze is math
the labyrinth language,
my vestibules sacked beyond recognition.

To imprint Zero on Eternity I must isolate silence first:
scry audible moments into openings, arias and sweeps:
frame faded dangers in the in-between of never–forever
where silence marks time with the tempo of geology.

On centrist pinhead a hard heart beats,
un-beats, reverses into diastole:
systolic recall slows return of sludge to well of soul.

In turbulent swirl unsteady hands on sandblast faces
fail to slow the passing stillness. Waking pressures exceed
capacity to hold such ph®ases accountable to single-word theories.

My nerves cannot staunch their own sodium,
such impulses calcify science of capture dissect & kill:
this latest arrival of the fittest erases any and all prior fealties.

What about the physicians of our futures,
attorneys attendant to the poor? Who will be left
to deliver their payload-dose of linnets? Who will debate
the refusal of leeches to latch onto next wave of amputations
now pharma bros have hightailed it west to Chicago?
Who holds, and who is holding?

Archangel heartbeats bore me to drink/drought, won't you throw
me an atlas please: let me choose my next but one battleground.
If the heart is a gas mask, propped stiff among the livid, where
pray tell will my own fluidity run free?

3.

cars crash into what we ground underground. silent slap of haptic wrist unites absence of aspiration. Banqiao. bounds of silence wound hard, burn deep in verse and signal eventual detection of our misconnection to earth. empty blue spaces between ice and sky ghost Gallic our spectacles. mothers, livid in solid state, flush men-of-war to bubble the surface: apparitions flicker their arrival between liquid & pre-emptives

3.

XVIII

Where does my fluidity lie?
What flushes jellyfish to surface-world:
knickers of silicon filtering ocean,
flowering and folding unto themselves?

Adaptable,
dimensional,
beckon turns breach to burn while pain
(price of transforming touch)
triggers hallelucinations.

There goes the fracking of vitreal gas,
shattering sedimentary bone.
Here are ossicles ringing imbalance
of my own innate vertiginous intent
:These are the bends to which I will go:

The nausea of near-poisonings is
retching chorus of chimeric ills,
until nothing is left to vomit up
but desiccant one-word notes

:SymptoM – mouthiest child,
embarrassment to disease –

fractures omertà of syndrome to tics, survives
repeat concussions of long-forgotten childhoods.
Silence tries
to live its own invention of a life,
sounds out implications of its latest sonic suicide,
feigns sleep until unconsciousness, pinned & pegged
to separate family-curse from myth-formulation.

On recovery:
Gorgon-haired bezoars hiss at knotted reflections;
gut remains key, intestines retain memories of meme.

Wolves batter on the door screaming …
"Little prig, little prig, let me go."

Visions, abandoned research ephemera,
bone blasphemous species till blasted and varnished
to slickest sheen. Skulls fuse sutures to burnish orifice
– *Innominatum Os* of the old machine.
Mentalists drown in coral reminders of
how they all were raised at sea: one of a perfect set of three:::
the firstborn safe eternal & still, the other free to oscillate
from restitution to reformate:::
One swaddles to Mother Octopus
while other chases jellyfish up

Will symptom out-parent disease,
be reasoned with,
be mature enough to see
the calculus cannot be rushed
until it's set in stone?

Just as paint escapes the brush, tones ascend
at moments of imperfect balance,
tiny expedients amplified
through shackling of acumen.

I thought a terrible thing to myself, then worried it to death:
which words steered me onto this ledge? My colour has run.
I hold no anatomy anymore, only shapeless suggestions yet,

I miss my appendix still – wigglin' appendage
ripped out and scrapped before learning what
it was for. Never to be reducible to my prime
again, these imitation-memes retrigger: the
jiggers, lost in transcription, code dots above
the *t*'s and crosses over the ayes.
My aye counts numbers
etched into and under my left-leaning ribs, those
sister-protectors wrapped round my pumphouse,
while, swaddled into my non-dom side, my lung
snores lazy and rough. No tongues of bone wrap

round my colon, unlovable li'l chute. No carapace
fronts the soft balloon that holds my limpid abdo
afloat. My sternum poses as storefront for heart,
while brain retains frackable shelves of skull. No
protection is offered to liver beyond cozying up
to attic of gut while clinging to lowest lying rung.
No tempting Darwinian twist will bind my offal
in chitin or organic armour: ~~Abode Abdomen~~
Madbone. Anagram, set my grammar free. Must
I be pliant enough to genuflect with skill or does
bending over save more lives than evolution ever
did? My kingdom for a corset: I'm sick to death
of sucking it in.
...
...
...
Instead of letting me geek it the chicken shoves
its head in my mouth and pecks at my tongue.
"Bite down," I always swore to myself, "I'll bite
down if a cock is ever shoved in my mouth."

I guess we all know different now – I'm not
cut out for carny work – and isn't that the nth
of the thing?

I ward off disease as easy as wax lips melt in sun.
My lipstick smears,
I'm cortex in a paper hat twerking muscle into fat.
Pull on my zippered spinal cord, click my heels and presto,
I magick myself to Planet Ganglion:
– synapse shadows
– welcome mat flickers
– stare at TV stare at radio stare at sun
– no fun since you left
– none since digital love is gone
– Onan's hand-off to Vulcan's beating-fist heart.

Monoliths hover over multiple locations.
Theories of pre-emptive strikes are apprised.
In the jealous house of rapturous mothers,
focus groups take offence at the word *appeared*,
preferring instead,
arrived.

what we know so far is …

4.

make it mine. make *Grandcamp* mine. make silence shout out at me. make wrist unite gag in purge and aspiration. make my own silence hard make it burn deep in verse and make me sign for the mis-directive over empty earth. make my spaces blue: make icy-ghost my spectacle sky. make mothers live their own lives, make men-of-war blush to surf the bubble apparatus. make flicker of film lick lies from streets, make dirt into another earth, make mimic silence the insomniac. make a heart reverse my potential to self is(h) beating

4.

XIX

It's a different world we greet
the moment we lay down in the street.

Walkers gawp at first; assume our outstretched arms
are hello-beacons to the monolith.

Officials ~~appear~~ arrive but we are well-dressed and white,
in no obvious distress, and breaking no city laws.

Strangers stream by on either side of the meat-islands
proffering limbs without flag or greeting.

Some pause to place flowers in hand, others weave charms
between bony fingers, tarnishing skin with cheap metals.

Children, discharged from hospital nearby, weave bravery-
beads through bracelets where charms would normally lie.

:Pots and pans bang overhead from cancer-ward balconies:

some nights their numbers are less than before, but
those who remain beat harder in show of undying support.

Children feed us until such time as concerns emerge
over sanitary conditions. No signage warns otherwise yet,

our mouths lie open for days at a time:

Leave a mouth open long enough,
someone will put something in it.

Physicians protest the feedings; prescribe fluids as flowers
have wilted and our mouths have filled with boli of mulch,

until a child pulls hard on a stiffening arm and one of us
swallows what's stuck in our throats. Vigil and loiter

turn swiftly to litter, the first tissue tossed
lands plump & full on the tongue. But one pump of the arm

sends dirty snubs south with nary a hint of obstruction.
Apple cores next, part rubbish part snack, then coffee

cups sandwich wrappers and fags, some quenched while
others still smoulder. In monolith-shadow, rumour has it

we are nothing but publicity stunts, some form of protest,
warnings minus a message. We swallow anything as long

as our arms remain lofty and lubricated. Many weeks pass.
No mention is made of defecation. What we know so far is

XX

:September posters stress personal details:

Our son has a mole beneath his left buttock,
My name is tattooed on my husband's arm,
Her hair was seven different colours today,

as if the missing were merely wanderers
lost dazed staggering toward identification
and ultimate repatriation, missing only the
kindness of recognition to be returned. we

shoegaze until feathers flutter overhead
and skies are scouted once again.

But look beyond the rubble.
Pause excavation and contemplate absence of
decomposition: our corrosion has taken to air.
We breathed you in for weeks but years will pass
before scans show shadow-growths, new lumps &
lesions for surgeons to slice & irradiate. They will

scorch our fields so their blades can ferry
steaming demons away: steam is the
meme of spirit's laughter, smoke is
spirit slaughter. Listen, please, I
still hear screams – Joan
from Accounts, Bill
from HR, Murray
in Security –
all begging, *Please,*
don't burn me again.
Abdulaziz, aviation enthusiast, awaits eternal
reward. All remains r remaindered: reminders
still remain. Pico-molecules gather in shadow
of breath to slowly re-emerge in first-trimester
ultrasounds in Manhattan, London's phoenixes

underground, Parisian eagles of death metal: all
grow where they are needed most. Their earliest
breaths are forever-wails, regaling snuffed-out
incarnations, arcade lovers of pixeled quark, a
minestrone of rhododendron, sex & rose tattoos
stirred into soup of birthmarks, silver-teeth and
chrome prostheses: miserable sudden vanishings
no multiverse can explain: no quantum-mania to
cutely shield their tiny weights till cavalry come.
From Hollow Men to Holocaust this *désolée* of
single cells (odourless tasteless senseless hell) is
divided into and by themselves – dreaming jellyfish
(oh, if only) – revisitant selves separate & replicate,
await rebirth through new noose of polka-dot tattoos

I would too

but my left leg made a wrong turn at the pelvis.
In spring my flowers sport yellow-blue bruises.
My bones, soaked in malice, are falsie-lymphatics
I only re-squeeze to be true. The soft-life to which
I cling dissolves the toughest parts of me: this is not
another why. Why more contrails than murmuration
overhead and, why, to walk where I breathe free and
full, must I drive to get there first? Why do I fantasize
neo-engine-hum of bumblebees – is it futile to splint
this word-cast of self-memed disease? Why do I rage
at clocks and hearts for steadily marking passing time?

5.

what we know so far is slapped haptics do
not prevent accidents. Vajont. Bikini Atoll.
our undergarments bind our aspirations
and wounds to each other, burn absence
of silence into our sleep to persist in
subliminal signals. the disconnect is
misdirection onto discrete paths, the will
to merge reveals our Gaelic ghosts have
wormed further into hearts smothered
gassed & unmasked: still-beating statues
amongst the living: no tide arrives, no blush
breasts the horizon flushed with cavalry
of men-of-war. on surface-world we bleat
about streets but usher in a different dirt.
we enter engine-hum of nature carrying
words on tiny hairs between the legs of
bees. the biology machines will rid us of
this obsession with words for disease.
pray we can switch to magic, pull cures
from formulae of the theories we knead

5.

XXI

Why rage at clock & heart for marking pass of time

I pray for magic and pull at invisible switches; plunge every organelle to its deepest freeze. The black curtain lowered over me is the other side of a mirror all gild & polish & fantasy. The plural of *fear* is *sphere*, can you see my magic run silent and dry, spent on the vine of self-serve toxins and cytokines?

The cell is dungeon and everything, but a ridge is rough-cut horizon stretched over the edges of the dizzying question: Do you see? The volatile shape of an atom's empty spaces is a silent eye filling in details, stepping into and out of shade, watching those looking in and sharing the vision but being the

thing while wondering what sits beneath the black curtain. *Cella* is Latin for *small door*, do you see: can you please just help me sleep? Pause the child who watches family crane onto their futures: paths, maps, memory loss (something to do with not enough water in middle age), maternal fevers: either

way it's like rain on the scalp of a newborn – beauty in context, obscene without – love's levering of microscopic lenses onto a drop of water; a film of sweat, a mounted slide of solitary tear. Sea monsters in the foreground of a light source so huge as to be nothing more or less than sky for as far as adjustable

eyes can see. This bivalent dream, the thresholds breached, are switches in me that flip in and out of reality, lucidity, reality, liquidity, reality, lividity till I stiffen and wake up half-dead perched on the edge of a binary blade held steady by something ancient caught in two minds for the first time in memory. I

am an unmercurial boy: decent trade for a thimble
of spit, a glistening vessel for odour and lingering
looks, run[a]way for takeouts & cast-off secretions.
This fortunate lamb, unfit to be tabled, casts up and
away from the body and bleedings on offer to lesser
men – sets to alter the empty again – follows making

of shapes to their drastic conclusions, carves stripes
on the skins: Begins Again. Don't pray, don't sing,
choose something. Be shepherd to sickly strangers'
sleep: ferry them through surgeries wipe memories
clean then pull their spirits back to most miraculous
recovery: let them redock themselves. So long since

I lost perspective on death after years of smelling
it on your breaths, on the linen & robes your loved
ones wrap you in before they brave home. Only then
do angel wing and furies beat. Your time is come and
I'm sorry that you're stuck with me but I put down
my drugs, unplug the electricity separating you from

me: I fold my palms around your cheeks, allow
myself to take you into parts of me. You flit & hover
amongst pagers & monitors bleating for too much
time already. Only now, as silence approaches, do
you listen like me: slowly deepening hums flatten
the air of a soul intent on sustaining itself. Darkness

shades into huddled shadows harried by sirens
alerting passersby that something here is trying to
die. Or maybe, the truth I'm fighting is that when I
wrote *I will be there when you die*, it might not just
have been for my wife but for some stranger's as yet
unborn child, and when that nightmare lands on
me, I will be there for you, not pausing the world so
I can sleep too: what we know so far is another world

XXII

where you keep telling me what this is not.
I have fevers,
                    you say it is not infection.
I am weary, bone-tired,
                                it is not deficiency.
I have pain where there was no injury.
I spasm but it does not come and go,
it is with me always yet,
                                nowhere to be seen:
no ion-ray no sonic beam can blast it into sight.

I waste away and still
                        it hangs invisible in the spaces
vacated by my meat.

I crack a joke – what we don't know can't kill me –
                        but this is no laughing matter now
(what doesn't kill me still knows where I live).

I grew accustomed to this being another part of me
but you say it is something I can no longer live with.

Have you forgotten already how you told me:
                                this isn't worth the worry,
                    most likely it's just in my head?

                        Now it's all we talk about,
                        the only thing I think about.
                            Do you think cure
                        will be word or formula

6.

:what we know so far is when we were unmade we were scrutinized to death. when we were cured we spun formulas for words. Exxon Horizon. slapstick mystics spit honeybees into our undergarments to buzz us in our sleep, burn us to forever-wounds, aspirate garlic from ghoulish hearts to gas the path toward mothers merging underwater with the past. the resistance of statues shames those with breath. deep beneath the horizon beats a different type of dirt, the grit of hope squeezed in flight to harbour pearl over pain memes and magic mutations: suffering solves nothing: prayer is no port: we can't exhume by digging the things we do not support:

6.

XXIII

Meme mutates to fulfill its abstractions?

If so, here's one for the word-horde:

If
Suffering = Pain + Resistance,
solve the equation for nothing.

Step One: Subtract resistance from both sides:
suffering – resistance = pain + resistance – resistance.
So,
suffering – resistance = pain ~~+ resistance – resistance~~.
Or,
reversing it so to speak,
to decrease pain, increase resistance.

Let's try again
::: (Suffering = Pain + Resistance) :::
This time, subtract pain AND resistance from both sides,
therefore,
suffering – pain – resistance
= ~~pain + resistance – pain –resistance~~
Or,
Suffering – Pain – Resistance = Zero.

Or …
if you remove pain and resistance from suffering,
you are left with nothing.

What we know so far is …

In a study of a wet nurse she is nothing. She left the baby
perched on the edge of a riverbank while she ran back and

forth to the twit in a hat singing Cole Porter tunes on
a swing set. While the baby is caught in the pregnant

pause between flying and floating dropping and drowning,
fleeing and squealing birds of prey are angled above

turning back to the bonnet on the bank like boomerangs
that dream of being tethered for once and for all, to lay

claim to the colours of flags of their choosing singing out
their adopted national anthem. They forget that fortune is

stitched into the belly of every newborn, their skin is
destined for glories greater than gumming up their guts.

Even though the space she found is better than her bearing
many have nevertheless remarked it is best to suggest

helpful advice to one with a brimful container than to
usher a mismatched knot into polite society. An easier

ploy is to figure out how one might trick her to forgetting
she was pulled out of reveries in the long grass by the

howls of a passing car. The gouge along the flank of
Governor Muybridge's chocolate Rolls sends *Dread*

Trotting down the spine of the governess every time she
pictures those pale legs pumping the air. She is not happy.

She is not entertained nor will she be contained by the
Jeeves and Wooster act of the fop on the swing and his

father, the governor, his wishes to remain discreet have
left her chained to the promise of her day in the sun like a

dog whose owner's head is buried in a bottle in an alley
nearby. She is noticed by many in passing, has been

known to leave someone else's man wrestling himself
with his dominant hand. She has been heard to state that

two men sleeping is better than one child wide awake in
her bed. She is not in need of a nurse or doctor to diagnose

a disorder, she is not in need of a priest to point out the
misdirect of her wicked ways, every night she wakes

screaming in invisible arms as the master's baby is swept
away by water with the coarse strokes of a hundred worn-

down brooms. She holds hard to the hands around her
neck, locks the chains one after another that rattle and

creak would she ever again consider tiptoeing to her gentle-
man's chamber from quarters down below. Each mirror

passed upon his landing is one of many Potemkin vistas
that reflect back frequent but steady journeys from

privileged birthrights to unmarked tombs ::: What we

know so far is … "poets elevate the presence of unlikely
secondary or background characters to heights of primary
importance in order to elucidate other themes. As such,
'She,' our primary character, 'is not contained'; she is

given a second life. However, the writer is not acting as
white knight here, he is simply repositioning the nurse
from 'tomb' to 'precipice,' where we, modern readers,
might use collective cultural wisdom to declare her fate …"

So, ~~in a study of a wet-nurse~~ **she is not**~~hing. She left the~~
~~baby~~ **perched on** ~~the edge of a riverbank while she ran~~

~~back and forth to the twit in a hat singing Cole Porter~~
~~tunes on~~ **a swing set.** ~~While the baby is~~ **caught in the**

~~pregnant~~ **pause between flying and** ~~floating dropping and~~
~~drowning,~~ **fleeing** ~~and squealing birds of prey are~~ **angled**

above ~~turning back to the bonnet on the bank like~~
boomerangs ~~that dream of being~~ **tethered** ~~for once and~~

~~for all, to lay claim~~ **to the colours of flags** ~~of their choosing~~
~~singing out their adopted national anthem. They forget that~~

~~fortune is~~ **stitched into** ~~the belly of every newborn, their~~
skin ~~is destined for glories greater than gumming up their~~

~~guts. Even~~ **though** ~~the~~ **space** ~~she found~~ **is** ~~better than her~~
~~bearing many have nevertheless re~~**marked** ~~it is best~~ **to**

suggest ~~helpful advice to one with~~ **a** ~~brimful~~ **container**
~~than to u~~**she**~~r a m~~**is**~~matched k~~**not** ~~into polite society. An~~

~~easier ploy is to~~ **figure** ~~out how one might trick her to for~~
getting ~~she was pulled~~ **out of** ~~reveries in the long grass by~~

~~the howls of~~ **a** ~~passing~~ **car**~~. The gouge along the flank of~~
~~Gover~~**nor Muybridge's** ~~chocolate Rolls sends~~ ***Dread***

Trotting ~~down the spine of the governess every time she~~
~~pictures those pale legs pumping the air. She is not happy.~~

She is not ~~entertained nor will she be~~ **contained** ~~by the~~
~~Jeeves and Wooster act of the fop on the swing and his~~

~~father, the gover~~**nor,** ~~h~~**is** ~~wis~~**he**~~s to remain discreet have~~
~~left her~~ **chained** ~~to the promise of her day in the sun~~ **like a**

dog whose owner~~'s head~~ **is buried** ~~in a bottle in an alley~~
nearby. She is not~~iced by many in passing, has been~~

~~known to leave some~~**one** ~~else's~~ **man wrestling** ~~himself~~
~~with his dominant hand. She has been heard to state that~~

two men sleeping ~~is better than one child wide awake in~~
~~her bed.~~ **She is not** ~~in need of~~ **a nurse** ~~or doctor to diagnose~~

~~a disorder, she is not in need of a priest to point out the~~
~~misdirect of her wicked ways, every night she wakes~~

screaming in invisible ~~arms as the master's baby is swept~~
~~away by water with the coarse strokes of a hundred worn~~

~~down b~~**rooms. She holds hard to** ~~the hands around her~~
~~neck, locks~~ **the chains** ~~one after another~~ **that** ~~rattle and~~

~~creak~~ **would** ~~she ever again consider~~ **tip**~~toeing to~~ **her**
~~gentleman's chamber~~ **from** ~~quarters down below. Each~~

~~mirror passed upon his landing is one of many~~ **Potemkin**
vistas ~~that reflect back frequent but steady journeys from~~

~~privileged birthrights~~ **to unmarked tombs** ::: What we

know so far is "this is not a revisionist work as much as a work of reclamation … **'she'** is afforded a narrative of her own. Reclamation allows a more nuanced look at the character, and in a sense, each character in sordid misogynistic pasts, as a means of providing us chance to airlift her from expectations politics, and into more informed, modern, ideally enlightened spotlight."

In ***A Study of a Study of a Nurse ...***

She is not perched on a swing set caught in the pause
between flying and fleeing, angled above boomerangs

tethered to the colours of flags stitched into her skin.
Though space is marked to suggest a container she is not

a figure getting out of a car nor Muybridge's *Dread*
Trotting. She is not contained nor is she chained like

a dog whose owner is buried nearby. She is not one man
wrestling two men sleeping. She is not a nurse screaming

in invisible rooms. She holds hard to the chain that would
tip her from Potemkin vistas to unmarked tombs ::: "This

poem is indicator of how far we have and haven't come.
The writer understands there is risk in revision & danger
in a lack thereof, as a study will reveal what is present, or
what can be observed, but a 'study of a study' will reveal
what has been missed. Yes, 'she' is left to the tipping but,
there is a 'chain,' and we can help to hold it, or release.

This poem is a chain. By magnifying her personhood, her
humanity, by show of what she is 'not,' rather than speak
for her, the writer makes the statement: 'how many "tombs
unmarked" could we exhume today by digging into what
we did "not" in the past?'"   What we know so far is ...

7.

when we were unmade we were scrutinized to death. when we were unmade we were words of and for wolves. we were unmade to churn out the latest millennium. this happens. once we were undergarments worn in sleep, bound forever to wrap ghosts of glass in swaddled pasts of second horizons, lilac hems of sky & sea, hope squeezed to hell in a shell of meme and mathematics: pain & suffering explain everything: prayer's port de bras digs into the armpit of what we did when the ratio of meme to mutation skewed

7.

XXIV

when we were unmade we were scrutinized to death. May-
be we should have been Marilyn but we arrived pre-abused
instead: star-crossed addicted a little bit nympho we trans-

form to robins above circular saws overlooking waterfalls.
Brushed ashore by current-flow and loneliest foghorns we
hung around to roll the girl over, were there when another

girl stumbled into town (fell down a mountain gripping
half a heart locket in one hand). The germ of a mole on a
teen is like half-heart lockets left in hock, flimsiest details

of a promise split into jagged approximation of haves and
half-knots, have and have to, twinkling terror of debutantes
in hand-me-down garters and hands off the goods. Such

clammy praise is plunging ache that scabs and scars but
never heals. The world is gone from velvet blue to blush-
ing bruise: here ends all the nerves. Small seeds of darkness

have taken root and there the synapse congeals: when old
wound heals the sun will reveal it, when healers fail the
dirt will conceal her. Nobody knows what she needs from

TV, we are absent mass at the centre watching the agents
chase the perverts. We are what killed what kept her living:
a most impotent agency, dualities beyond make-believe,

terrible doubles making trouble for everybody concerned.
Theirs is a fury asking old questions of soft new flesh, Will
he come for me next when he's done with her? What we

know for sure is: No, you're safe, you are men: next will
be another woman, a blond in high school using drugs
and crying out for help who delivers abundances of food

but never eats herself. She is half the high school girls we
know, but all her family's daughters. If only we could all
be little girls awhile, holding hands inside the clocks but

we are weeds instead when we could have been timeless
trees, garmonbozia wrapped in plastic holding fast to the
inert darkness pressing tiring robins onto spinning blades.

XXV

What We Know So Far Is

I stink of early guilt. The swell of first blood opens older
wounds in skin. Limbs that stir the pus – blood-borne and
hemo-erotic to hers – twist flesh slow to unwound. Drawn

to stand like tulpas hobbled & tamed without tether, ribs
of furies spring up & out of ever-evolving crucifictions:
though dirt scents genuine under nail she smells me still.

She races over & back again from peak of one dangerous
man to the other, hollowing her valley of safety between.
Pandora. Papancha. Pontypool. Night of Dawn of Day of

Age of the Living Dead the Dead the Dead. Aquarius!
When beauty bites down, perfect teeth disclose collusion
and novel incisions. Nothing thrives on the steps of trans-

ition: what little grows sits wrong like hair on sewer pipes.
This thing is the same everything until everything is done
changing – volatile outlines converting heather to heathen

cavorting as gooseflesh copse and goose-stepping corpse.

What appeals to the taste of us in our mouths is hope of
perfect timing flawed: eruptions, collapses, destructions
lodged between crown & molar, grinding the collective,

yet our desperation hisses from roots resistant to the re-
routine and all for the want of a ring of unbroken salt
around the world. Even as beauty bites down hard and

routine bites right back again the heart remains a pulsatile
sun, pyramid of bone, throbbing glove: planet-womb. Sun
Glove Womb. We should be warm; warm as Eden minus

the honeytrap of hot cider: Confusion in her eyes says it
all, it's about Apple, never about Eve, this will inform our
needs to know. We have lost control again. This perpetual

motion of falling asleep on the edge of unknowing is
tailor-made to forget the meme, error that ricochets for
years between cold doorsteps and strangers' weather.

Make fog your screen, flee when least expected to. Do not
turn every rock over, remember sand is dug & poured.
The chirrup of nerve, half-shuttered half-frayed, reminds

how loss of time can throb as sinking clocks cling on one-
handed while the other points out how we might all be
saved but never again rewound. Does our knowing of this

mark firmer the will to deny the psychic drivers? Invasion
poses as intervention, transplants set as institution, skill sets
merge to sweep immunity under hair & skin, between flap

& tongue. Under every rock, an overhang of man-shadow
veils flora cordoned into grids, home to black-boned birds
that cough up rough & yet with pure intent hop on & caw

from mound to rock, beckoning begging, *"Here, caw, here,
you dig? Here, is where he poured her."* Meme don't fail
me now: forgive me ye sinners for I have fathered filthy

strangers on haunted box springs and grimly laundered
sheets. Such moments persist in galaxies so tiny as to spin
between inspiration. Quasi-silence breathes in light un-

dimmed to pulse beyond grasp of pixels: shadows hang
in drying dust. New lures hide the happenstance that only
mothers betray, loose-fit concept anyhow hung low on

family tree of strays while lazy words repropagate – the
rate of which potentiates till loose phrases come together
and blur the centre line. Hold up any page, the Rorschach-

shape of ink makes pools beneath to blot the blind of our
memories out. Bloodstains in the basement whisper word-
hoards in the grout: they've stopped sounding off: the rate

of meme accelerates … begins to churn mutations out.

8.

what we know so far is we need a pause, Deepwater Valdez. Port of Beirut. so many generations unmade with a word even though the oirish have no word for *no* even though the plural of *word* is *sword* and will be for another millennium at this rate of imitation. those born only to sleep forever are worn for weeks swaddled in the hems of women until the first horizon is passed. the second is only seen from the beach through spiral shells once every few thousand years

8.

XXVI

What we know so far is the Irish word for *Irish* is *Gaelic*,
Gaeilge, but after a thousand years the English still call

me *Paddy* – my father's name (which also means white
in pachuco). Voznesensky taught me Russian for *no* is *hac*,

My fathers taught me no Irish equivalent exists. We say, *ní*
hea instead; *it is not*. You ask if I am a poet, I cannot say no

so instead I concede I am not. Maybe it's in the way they
wrangle the truth, force my own tongue from my mouth,

that the word still sticks – *hack*, the only sound to come out.

The Irish for *shadow*, *scáth*, is also our word for *shelter*:

the crows warn scáth scáth, shelter in shadow, maybe we
should turn every rock over: tell bell bird harp & star, Quiet,

you! No wonder they all hate poetry: the poet, not the priest,
is true vassal of heaven. Our words are simple music yet

the rules are fancy affect to most. If assonance & cadence
are foundation enough for poetry, play Dublin songs for all

involved: Dublin Doubloon City of Moonz Wake the Devil,
tell him Moon is up. Women, draw down & gather power

enough to mould monsters into birds. Furies, fury of seas,
like Galilee flowing to Thessaly: these are the cellar doors

of my youth, their downward elisions – GAH LIH LEE –
THEH SAH LEE – do-re-mi's through smooth transition

of vowelled sibilants. Consonants count no greater worth
than fettered swings from which my sweetest vowels sing.

Open the cellar door to Thessaly from Nazareth to Galilee.
Lazarus begs the godchild, Please, Lord, will you finally

reconsider & re-dead me: pray silence this stuttering sprite.
Thessaly, Galilee, euphonies license the whisperings of my

comfortable glees. While Black Speech & blasphony cough
the onomatopoeia of Dachau up, spit Slytherin of Auschwitz

out, we choke on the raw staccato of scratched-up scalps,
butcher-shorn with blunted tongs. Skittish and shrill they

shit the page with self-implication – Hac. Hac: they take it
all back – scour the paint job of cellar door with one ugly

consonant after another, splashed out in tall-Man whitewash
letters – No Dogs No Blacks No Irish: Thank you for that …

what we know so far is
One score before Gettysburg a third of my people starved
at home before another third took flight by sea. To the west

men could fish at least but inland souls had come to know
that nothing to harvest meant nothing to sell meant nothing

to eat meant nothing to grow: nothing but Hungry Grass in
escrow. Wherever a famine victim fell, a patch of Hungry

Grass would swell. To tread on it cursed you to starve to
death in minutes which is why elders carry crusts of bread

in their pockets: not for ducks or pigeons or beggars but as
antidote to Hungry Grass: no danger lies on our concrete

streets but mind you care when crossing fields. Westward
over the ocean a generation made land at last, where many

were handed a musket in lieu of promised citizenry: some
received powder while others took shot. Those who begged

fortune and prayer watch over them through famine, storms
and dysentery, bayonet and artillery, now fingered the fields

for balls of steel beneath their stricken brothers until, BAM,
like that, we're digging in the dirt for our paddy-lives again.

But this is no ordinary paddy field, for as Brendan Behan
told me, "Ireland's a village – spread to Trieste with Joyce,

Devon and O'Casey, Paris and Beckett. Ireland – a figment
of Anglo-Saxon imagination … a lie, a non-existent state."

It's a long way to go. The innocents wait on their shadows'
return from where they are frightened to stray themselves.

Our bravest & most desperate set sail to halve our starving
load, survived as punch bags & punchlines abroad for want

of a fucking potato.   Yet, from what we now know of our
own lost tongue, Gaelic's root is the same as that for sauce

[garlic, antidote to vampires]; generations simmered & boiled
to season the taste of our flaws when, sometimes, all we need

is a pause

XXVII

when we are played are we plucked or blown, are we strummed and
our nethers feathered?

When we are played everyone knows but no one ever speaks,
no one is seen to intervene yet no one fails to get footage.

None pray over those who sleep easy: none skirt fields on chirping feet
toward silence of anchored home where pillows and sheets house exit wounds.

Let's prepare for farewells first by honouring elder hearts –
those flues of wasted pressure hissing underneath our sterna.

Should we bleed the elderly gradual like flues of wasted pressure,
hissing under everyman moments redirecting us home where
pillows and sheets house exit wounds?

Let's taste the sometime nourishing hook for none pray over those who sleep easy.
None skirt fields on indecision to clump like thrombus instead:
everyone speaks and no one knows.

Might we bleed gradual elder hearts,
pump valves before scenes of feeding our parents converge;
everyman moment which turns us accomplice acquitter eventual all?

That which avoids the hook is tasted yet, it is sometimes nourished too.
Family gathers at the crotch of every decision; comes together like platelets,
like cold soup dribbles from chin to schlup and drips to pool

so those of us struck dumb might look within to scry. To carry on regardless
would ignore how tiring blood which drives us forward
will one day choke our engines dry.

Do I draft Rx for my sorry PRN or best leave unresolved?
Understand: THIS is what you will always forget me for,
random fractured consecular thoughts: to feed or feed not, forgive

forgive not. These are questions in front and behind me, word-castes
formed to splint my disease, soft-focus poems grafted to virus touted
as new ideas. Each splinter is implicature, i.e., it's the right number

AND the wrong word – other wor(l)ds perhaps but not in this one –
i.e., slow feet of sleep, the click the ricochet the leap, the change in
gait from help to heel – new onset chorea of dance, a choreography

of chance – triple helix of father son & holy ghost, Laius Oedipus
platypus ... Freud: vivisecting interzone of eels before wading into
our psyches – slick tissue split to reveal phallus of the phallus of the

reeds, nested gonads giving in to theories proofed one fondle
at a time. The tightrope from science to sacrilege and back,
mimics tension of telomere's signal – bug-eyed chromosome

– tail and claws: this too is not the pause but DNA's checkered
flag where lineage falls and defers to disrepair. Here is where we
die away: here is where we reincarnate to second skeins of

amateur dramatics, third dream of dimming silver screens,
sally forth on gilded reminiscence of faded filth stars. Skin
up with partner & starlet alike, decant experience to de-frame

the posters, strip the veneer as sitters ripple and glisten because to
spherical eyes such pictures frame the risks we take to underwrite
the money we'll make analyzing dreams – better work than sifting

through the gonads of eels: in this museum the exhibits see you too.

What we know so far is

In Texas State mental facility, technicians drain formalin from jars

that house brains for posterity. The exposed bellum is wrapped in

cheesecloth, which can also be used to separate curds from whey.

In lithography it mops up gum-Arabic. When soaked in rum and

wrapped 'round fruitcake dough, cheesecloth nurses the raw mix as it sweetens toward the ripening. In séance & channellings, cheesecloth pulled off illusions of ectoplasmic otherlys. Cheesecloth inhibits desiccation too and, like curds, binds dead tissue together. Preserved poutines of cerebral hemispheres are dusted with thousands of tiny filaments: worn eyelashes of finely shredded parmesan. An unsalted German cheese, made with centuries' old recipe, is called a quark. While Texan technicians resoak brains in fresh new formalin the cheesecloth is pegged up to air-dry and bleed. Parmesan. Quarks. Ectoplasm: each cling to cloth like secrets caught in history's net

9.

so far, what we are sorry for is unresolved
despite the pause despite Deepwater Valdez
despite Port of Beirut despite so many
generations unmade with a word and even
though the oirish have no word for *no* even
though the plural of *word* is *sword* and will
be for millennia at this rate of mutation-
imitation those born to only sleep forever
are worn for weeks in swaddled hems
until we reach the triptych of sea sky &
beach, sat still in perfect shirtless circles,
and unstitch sleep from skin, set loose
the bloodlust of a thousand piercings

9.

XXVIII

until it's like listening to a fucking headache again, sat there posing questions to myself like Beckett Waiting on Bacon

Like man unbuttoned in sparest landscape

– like man in cricket pads, draped in purplish shadow,
rising toward body-traitor-parks
– like picador-form at window, crouched in study
of curtained nudes
– like bathtub reflecting on mirror
– like man on mail-order rowing machine,
staring at blind cord overhead
– like man eating legs of chair,
flapping about on fainting couch
– like man pulling door behind him
– like man walking man drinking man working in fields
– like men wrestling behind sand dunes
in long-bladed grass
– like man with camera
– like man talking at work
– like man and obstruction
– like man running water into and out of taps
– like man chopping at his own tides
– like man's motion denied in afterthought
– like man bloating, man turning over
– like man sees man spirit-reading
seated in silence
– like man not mouthing words to himself
– like man not turning pages
– like man not thinking lest sound is made
– like reflexively ignoring signals
lumbaring round the back
to massage kneadiness of prayer into gaps
between membrane and innominatum vein
– like here are two brick lobes:
Rosencrantz & Guildenstern,

struck dumb for once
now nothing has already happened twice
– like limbo light of nearly night
basking in spectra of silence from red's resilience
to violet's violence & everything lit up between
– like two half-hearts of a ghosted hole
bent on remerging dependently
– like two intimations of new life
re-enacting the game of survival
where every absolute is prized:
winner leaves other world behind.

XXIX

What we know so far is one calls out across the ocean,
another pushes sky away.

Space is formed in barometer's forge of pain and separation.
For those who shed memory of gravity

the cave they project is portal granting entry to our homes.
He tasks himself with replacing bones

in the meat of those who come to meet him broken. He pulls
at leaves that sprout from deep

within his sleeves, offers one to those who've lost the will
to sing or speak: like the woman who

flew over forest fire to hear her favourite song: like the boy
who doesn't know if he's ever been in

love: like the man, a Tom Waits tribute act, whose heart
stopped during the second verse of

"I Don't Wanna Grow Up." Like the woman, immaculate in
Chanel, whose mother killed her father

and doesn't remember the act. She asks her daughter daily
where her husband has gone, who has

he left her for? She asks him a question no one should
address yet he does and we agree that

there's a slippery ease with which we all re-steer into grief.
As he takes his leave a final flower falls

from his sleeve, flutters to the stage. The plucked wing, the
skeleton spent, is farewell performance

to die for. Later, at home, I open a chimney into my neck to
ladder a signal and smoke stragglers out.

It's official, cancer meme is viral now, like whispered
opportunities [foreign possibilities] to

cells long-accustomed to settling for less but reprogrammed
instead to embrace the false caress that

fosters metastatic egress. They overwhelm dendritic web,
trigger ganglionic excess. Remote connections

ring mycotic to all illogical ends – train lazy lung blow old
smoke away – teach swelling brain

the pulsatility of pride. The transplant tongues its older gums,
clucks wet against the turbulence of

children coming to blows over trivials like burial clothes,
ill-fit with tags clipped round the back

like the label looped 'round Father's toes. Cancer has a new
motto: bring an appetite, bro.

Monolithic inf[l]ections aren't spread through tainted food
but opportunistic contaminants instead

as typically found in spoken wounds – public shaming and
ill-wisher wells, hate speech, pile ons:

all viral memes. The infected, the he[a]rd, are coveted by
street gangs. They train them as speakers,

line them up as sonic tags, markers of power and territory:
better still if the infected are white. Non-

sense phrases are sprayed on the cages as stark reminders
to look up and read – speak loud the wounding

words. Me-me owns these streets. First law of this world:
all are hungry. Second: everything's horny.

Third: nobody's made it this far. In other news tonight: five
kids biked to the woods to play at *Stranger Things*;

one did not return. A single victim means anything,

multiples point to white male until proven otherwise

:Take the Hatter's *t* away, a thirsty Hater takes his place:

what we know so far is

Bitten is not the same as eaten: this meme is not on me.

Sometimes a man tumbles down steps glancing over his

shoulder at the peaks of his trajectory. He measures his

mass in coin, surprises even himself. His sand and bone

refract his meat so, invisible, he learns how he fits this

world. He drinks to the day his mother left, set out as any

creature might, drawn to places they hunted & ate – pain

burrows deep while the cubs go hungry. Faitheists teach

best how to praise, let falling man appraise the preacher,

whisper plans without him into bleeding ears at the feet of

never-ending stairs. He circles for months in the struts of

his mother's wagon oblivious to coming explosive release,

arrives just in time to purge her of him and everything his.

Losing her song is his cobbling to tectonic screams. Plates

shift, forests wilt, islands sink. Gathering drought is enough to drive some drinkers crazy. The sick are quickly devoured upon entering the clinic, their wellness too threadbare a rug to cover the souls of tired feats. Meme manoeuvres essential angle to picket collection of new-world commandments. The fight drains late into day, peters out on most ordinary morning – mountaintop blood boils up and over only to cool and steep like so much tea. I try writing life with my reading hand, bid easy on nothings, imagine they'll one day make book. Some beautiful mornings I get what I want, I hover tile-naked work-ready in the coolest good nights of whenever; best lines quieten the war between sex & planet, gristle & vegetable as Lagrange spins out over mausoleums and souls to fill graveyards with my unwritten books. Nobody speaks the thing while listening out for what's being said elsewhere, leaving room for words to squeeze inside those wounds as yet unseen. My route to their underworld is through the roots of family – that blaze beyond stars and Son fired by Gods & young. "Don't budge," I warn while soaring past, "hold fast and face your firing squads when bulls-eyed in clearing of mirrors: the shadow is as before. Light makes good your escape so spin hard in this circle while the boundary's got your back. Run to the statue of moonrise pool where circles come to resume before diving into starrier seas." On the underside of the world my day is neatly tucked away. Bedtime stories dangle overhead like mobile nooses and me all upside-down. My toes replace my frown which, wrong way round, is now a grin. The songs begin: Who planted us? Who planeted us? How long have I plunged in upturned arbour? I cut me free and roots run from my head through beards of dreams connectined to my re-souled feet. My silence takes shape, pockets shade for later; my sunset is Enneagram colour chart tracing pigment one through nine, line of dissolving cubes attesting to who was here when the ink ran dry. Maybe it's as it should be that I abandon my figments one leaf at a time, still I shelter under the fin of feather and wing that softens chrome of limb and angle of exposed collarbone. This could be choreography of my long-rehearsed obituary but now I'm rallying to spoil it all. I emerge from tattoos of ancient worlds on the underbelly of a pregnant whale – gravid atlas bucking every time she breaks the surface. Absent nations ripple a torso where countless calves were nursed and nap in amniotic underworlds. Each wrinkle a slice of undecipherable message, every scar is notch of war, a useless mé féin (me too) gouged with thimble of chum in the churning scum of a mouth-breathing ocean dweller swallowing tiny creatures whole: vessel harpoon buffoon and all. The living ink from deep within taints mother's skin with the blood of a thousand piercings. Again, bitten is never the same as eaten. The sharp-snouted day frog is extinct (chytrid fungus to blame): thickened skin is observed as nutrients are no longer absorbed and toxins no longer repelled. Seizures come late as does loss of the righting-reflex – vestibular response that resets orientation when posture is suddenly changed. Somatosensory inputs reroute and re-form cerebellar references to scan back and forth between actual and expected then correct for the difference between. When a cat falls it turns its head and spine to realign its lower half and always lands upright. This reflex is present in healthy babies from eight to ten weeks. Early pregnancy tests date back to ancient Greece when sacks of wheat were watered with a pregnant woman's urine and germination confirmed expectancy. In the 1930s, researchers injected gravid urine into *Xenopus* frogs then floated the specimen in water: if eggs were found in the fluid this also confirmed another mother-to-be. The market in *Xenopus* frogs exploded and drove them to the ledge of near extinction. A different *Xenopus* species is the perfect model for developmental biology: modelling human disease and birth defects, as well as basic science and toxicology of cancers. Interferon – interzone of signal-proteins – is produced in response to many viruses: symptoms of infection such as fever and myalgia are a result of interferon production, while COVID-severity correlates with older age and increased population of interferon-producing cells. In tadpoles, bio-augmentation is used to treat chytrid infections: animal & ecosystem are both treated with probiotica to express antifungal metabolites mooted to cure disease. Too late, alas, for the sharp-snouted frog who knows nothing of cellular division nor the aspirations of pregnant women. What we know so far is we skirt our ignorance of the nucleus, risk neighbouring violence to circumvent in deathly silence. I reread my own mutation's announcement to diagnose myself one of many redundant sells of self-replication. Separation sums this instability of my own moment; neo-silence is near antidote to time spent anchoring continuity as unknown pasts & mergent futures hide in soundless vibrant hums. The artificial why I hold to be true is an unravelling violence of slowly tightening knots. When we retrace our steps through time to arrive at single corporeum will we reject our own mergings, toss offer of transplant back in favour of natural harvest? If we truly believe ghosts leave footprints which retreat in the wrong direction, maybe discrete paths will converge on those most revealing and vulnerable parts of us.

XXX

the Irish for *truth* is *firinne* (fear in ya), what else do we need to know? except *eaten* is the same as *bitten* and the plural of *mitten* is *smitten.* the phonetic Irish for *truth* is *fear in you* and the blood of a thousand piercings collects in perfect little circles. the plural of *leap* is *sleep*, unstitching skin to swaddle triptych of sea sky and beach. at current rate of mutation the Gaelic for *no* will soon be born. a generation sworn to sit repentant by the banks of deep bodies of water resolves to storm horizon instead in squadrons of twos and threes. clear passage appears every thousand years through golden-spiral equations spun through tiny shells sewn into the hems of forever sleepers. the plural of *whorl* is *swirl.* current horizon might hold out for weeks. the plural of *word* is *sword* once ratios have wandered askew. beachfront prayer digs deep in dirt with crossed hands and manicured fingertips. the plural of *pear* is *spear.* the plural of *leap* is *sleep.* second horizon hems lilac lisp between sky & sea. swaddled ghosts of glass burn up sand to scrabble for oysters in undergarments reserved for pilgrims. suffering explains everything. everything is re-unmade

when we were wolves we were unmade. when we were words we were unmade. we cannot un-exhume by excavating what we never dug. prayer is no longer a port, its plural is *sport.* nothing outlasts suffering. no jewel trumps pain, no magic holds mutation hobbled mid-flight turning memes into sunken statues. underwater mothers merge as choral reefs to aspirate gas from ghoulish hearts to bind wounds on souls of our feet to churn us to death in our sleep. stings are plucked like death yanks cures from theories, redacts remedies, pockets keys to the apothecary. the plural of *cure* is *skewer.* when we are cured we will become formula – new format for words we unmade to replace the words we scrutinized to learn how to pray so we might sate our death-obsession. let's switch to magic of biology-machines, send messages woven in tiny hairs on the hind legs of bees. get the word out: rid us of disease. re-enter the engine-hum of nature, usher different dirt from the bleats of sheepish streets. no blush breasts the horizons, no cavalry flush with men-of-war goes OTT. the plural of *men* is *menses*, or *semen*. no tide arrives at surface world while beating-heart statues walk beside the living regaling Gaelic ghosts with words worming deeper into hearts. the plural of *mother* is *smother*, gas is unmasked to the will of discon-necti(o)n to tight-fisted push of protein's misdirecti(o)n onto discrete paths burned into the absence of silence during sleep. signals persist. subliminal haptics do not prevent accidents. holstered clocks mark fury of night and heart. beaten potential is harsh reversal of insomnia through silence to meme. make dirt into another earth, lick lies from streets, make men of our blushing surfers, make men of our surface-bubblers with the same apparatus that makes mothers unroll their own sleeves. make ghosts of ice make spectre make spectacle make my species blue. the plural of *verse* is *versus*, make your cut deep in this body of work, make me sign off on my own expenses, make this mis-directive of empty earth make my own silence hard enough to make wrists unite with pelvic maps. make aspirations gag in the purge. make silence all about me. the plural of *pout* is *spout*, make me grand and camp. the plural of *camp* is *scamp.* make me solid and stiff make me bested and livid in the lay of lands of gas. gas smothers liquid, solid breathes gas, liquid shits solid-state. paddy crosses dry ice with extinct frogs to frame pregnant vacuums at the heart of haunted spectacle. time disconnects binding from ground as final signal redirects what we used to know through filter of dust-aspirations burn-wound scars and silent wrists, slapped universes and cars crashed into monoliths. connectin hollows in-between-self of merge and rejection, grinds ground into blue dust to sprinkle beneath us above elysian icefields. the plural of *no* is *snow.* cars crash into absence of background hum, leaves me light-headed & rubbled in cloth until I am buried beneath concrete tongue with offerings. the plural of *tongue* is *stung,* swelling & judged rough, pressing raw on every nerve the recoding of red-herring DNA. escape the cave, arms overflowing with rubbish – Gaimans Gandalfs Salmans Siams – plural of *ever* is *sever* so yes dissect my dream of vinyl paper pets, solid liquid gas, from the neck of my articulated self. nothing universal happens through good will or haptic alone. Omagh. Hiroshima. wrist-slaps. car crashes. scar-rashes. what we know so far is

10.

10.

Notes

This book is influenced by anything and everything I have consciously/unconsciously soaked up through most if not all of my sentience to date. One example: Saturday, November 1, 2024, while riffing with Cal at/of Sellers & Newel I started raving about Sun Kil Moon's song "Richard Ramirez Died Today of Natural Causes." Later, while driving home, the song shuffled onto my hands-free A**le CarPlay system and I remembered how the song's stream-of-consciousness (but actual meticulous language-construction & lyricism) is something I promised myself I would one day attempt. Another example is the Hal Hartley film *Henry Fool*, in which the Simon Grim character compulsively writes a long poem that provokes visceral, sometimes violent, reactions from everyone who reads it. We never see or hear a single word of the poem but every time I sit down to write I am trying to create that exact poem for those exact reasons. There will be other examples tomorrow, but the following spring to mind during the final edit of this poem today …

Nulla

The italicized quote is from the story "The Hole" by Hassan Blasim, from his collection *The Corpse Exhibition: And Other Stories of Iraq* (Penguin, 2014).

I

The hip or pelvic bone, os innominatum, was so named because it "did not resemble another thing," this at a time when anatomical nomenclature was based on what a body part most resembled, e.g., *scapula*, shovel/trowel; *trapezoid*, obv.

III

Fómhar, pronounced Foe-vur.

Elvi, plural of Elvis.

VI

Happened in a hospital in Dublin on the threshold of commencing organ donation / transplantation: delayed the procedure by two hours.

VIII

Ontario burns but I live by the lakefront. I'm channeling "London Calling" by The Clash.

Lewy bodies . . . family tree. In recent years, many friends and family members have experienced dementia, Alzheimer's or otherwise, not least my wife's father, Jean-Paul Jeudy; my friend Peter Rakaric's father and so many besides. It's devastating and it terrifies me that one day this may well be my own fate . . .

X

An elaboration on part of *Nulla* (so named because there is no Roman numeral for zero).

XII

Contains references to the above/ground press chapbook *In the Museum.*

1.

Oklahoma! is used as safe word here, not as reference to the musical. Whenever I think of Omagh, I want to scream, *Uncle, Pineapple* or something far more obscene.

XIII–XIIIb

Science.

2.

Seveso, Italy, 1976.

XIV

Taibhse, pronounced Thow-ish-ah.

Taibhseach, pronounced thow-ih-shook.

Taibhsím, pronounced thow-ih-sheem.

XV

Lots of musical references here: band names, song titles, etc., with hope that proximity to music will make the work more lyrical.

XVI

In celestial mechanics, LaGrange points are points of equilibrium for small-mass objects under the gravitational influence of two massive orbiting bodies. Mathematically, this involves the solution of the restricted three-body problem. *Written well before and in complete ignorance of the Netflix show of the same name: no such thing as an original idea but I do believe in a theory coming into its own and entering the general (sub)consciousness; how else to explain BOTH *Deep Impact* and *Armageddon*?

Joy, selfish act of resistance, re-circumscribes / to Oi, itself an act of brutishness is reference to the Colossus (wink) that is the British band Idles.

XVII

What about the physicians of our futures is a blatant self-referential shout-out from *This Insistent List* (ThreadNeedle Publications); as too is *If the heart is a gas mask.*

Linnets (Larry Levis, whom I learned of through James Lindsay).

I'm pretty sure there's a Pixies reference in this section too.

3.

Banqiao Reservoir Dam, 1975.

XVIII

Yes, I make up words like *hallelucinations* (and *crucifictions*). Don't ruin it for me.

Contains the best Three Little Pigs pun I am aware of; prove me wrong.

I have long held that the abdomen is a spectacular failure in terms of functional design.

Bite down is more *Geek Love* than *Shawshank Redemption.*

4.
SS *Grandcamp*, Texas City, Texas, 1947.

XIX

Obsessed as I am with Radiohead and the many amazing videos that accompany their music, this is a blatant rip-off of their "Just" video (dir. Jamie Thraves), with maybe a tiny *Walking Dead* reference thrown in (not for the last time), and early COVID-lockdown public happenings such as when citizens applauded frontline health care workers at 7:00 p.m. with pots and pans.

XX

Hmmmmm, 9/11, Ukraine and my eternal battle with parasomnia.

5.
Vajont Dam, Italy, 1963.

Bikini Atoll, 1945–58.

XXI

"A Little Peace and Quiet," September 1985, *Twilight Zone* TV Series.

Cellar Door: phonesthetic term referenced by Drew Barrymore's character in *Donnie Darko.*

Contains personal references to too many nights to count spent in various intensive care units in the graceful embrace of innumerable ICU nurses accepting the spiritual inevitable and ushering souls toward peace and dignified ends: specifically thinking of Chantal (RIP) holding a dying day-old baby at 6:00 a.m., looking at me and saying, *We are the parents she needs right now.* Fuck.

XXII

Not aimed at anyone in particular at all, just a general observation.

6.
Duh.

XXIII

Inspired by Jenni Offill's *Weather*, and latest excuse to go cryptocounting again.

"Crytpocounters" was the first poem I published (*The Fiddlehead*, Winter 2015) and the subject of my *Ampersand Review* Contest shortlisted essay "Control."

This section also contains one of my two long-running in-jokes, whereby I find new ways to include the poem "A Study of a Study of a Nurse from the Battleship Potemkin" in almost every book I publish. So far, it has appeared in the chapbook *Safe Spaces*; my debut poetry collection, *Recovery Community*; and the next thing I do after this. I do, however, insist on mixing it up each time, in this instance creating a short prose piece that I erasure and intersperse with comments from bird, buried press, an online poem critique project of Justin Million who rejected my chapbook of the time but was gracious enough to feature this poem as their inauguration online posting in April 2018. To this day, I am proud of how this discussion of my poem enhanced what I thought I had achieved purely by instinct and accident. It highlights also, for me at least, the vital importance of outside discussion and consideration of one's work.

7.
Piper Alpha, Scotland, 1988.

SS *Mont-Blanc*, Halifax, 1917.

XXIV

An update of "Participation and Passive Views (*Twin Peaks* in Under Two Minutes)": 2nd Place, 2019 *Vallum* Award for Poetry.

XXV

Starts off by referencing multiple zombie movies before intertwining lyrics from Joy Division's "Love Will Tear Us Apart" and "She's Lost Control."

Strangers' weather is a direct reference to a line in a poem featured in *The Next Wave: An Anthology of 21st Century Canadian Poetry* (Anstruther Books/ Palimpsest Press, 2018), but I can no longer remember the precise reference or poet, nor can I locate my notes: Sorry.

Many references also from the ThreadNeedle poetry collection *This Insistent List.*

XXVI
True story.

Paddy, pronounced pah-dee.

Scáth, pronounced scaw.

XXVII
Sorry folks, it's not true.

9.
Deepwater Valdez, even Marky Mark gets this one.

XXVIII
Waiting for Godot meets Francis Bacon meets Tom Stoppard.

XXIX
A fragment written on the drive home after Nick Cave's solo show at University of Toronto's Convocation Hall, September 30, 2019; the last show we attended before the first lockdown.

Walking Dead meets *The Wire*.

More science, and the righting reflex (why cats "always land on their feet").

XXX
The plural of *wine* is *swine*.

10.
This is what it is not – a palimpsest – all of *What We Know So Far Is …* written over itself.

Acknowledgements

This book began by riffing back and forth with the wonderful Jim Johnstone through early drafts. Without Jim, I would not have had the place or nerve to do what I try to do with words.

This book was plucked from the pile by Paul Vermeersch, who proceeded to jolly roger it within an inch of its sanity. Paul's editing of this poem was an education for me in how to push, prod and gently provoke. Paul made me go there again and again.

To Noelle and everyone at W&W, thank you for this beautiful publishing experience.

To the Mc Donnells, Jeudys, O'Donnells, Fallons, Tomlinsons, Rastogis, Gilmers, Mahas & Yous of this world: *I don't know where it comes from.*

To Audrey, Cillian, Patrice, Pat & Paddy, Jean-Paul & Josette: Love Love Bloody-Nose Love.

Dr. Conor Mc Donnell is a poet and physician at the Hospital for Sick Children, Toronto. He is the author of two collections of poems (most recently, *This Insistent List*) and three chapbooks. His poetry has appeared in various Canadian and international publications, as well as noted medical journals such as *JAMA* and *CMAJ*. He is an associate professor at the University of Toronto and editor-in-chief of *Case Repertory*, a Narrative-Based Medicine Lab publication that seeks to engage and promote the voice of the patient in collaboration with their health-carers. He is a frequently invited international lecturer on pediatric perioperative care, error prevention and opioid stewardship, and he is current vice-president of the Canadian Pediatric Anesthesia Society. Conor works weekends at Sellers & Newel Second-Hand Books in Little Italy, Toronto, where they have words for people like him.